A Sense of Time

Poems and Antipoems
1969 — 1972

Raymond Garlick

MCMLXXII

GWASG GOMER

First Impression - June 1972

© RAYMOND GARLICK, 1972

SBN 85088 146 3

Published by Gwasg Gomer
with the support of The Welsh Arts Council

Set in Monotype 12 on 14pt Bembo. Printed on Glastonbury Antique Laid

Designed and Printed in Wales by J. D. Lewis and Sons Limited
at Gwasg Gomer, Llandysul in the County of Cardigan.

ER COF AM
WALDO
PRIFARDD
HEN GYFAILL

Many of these poems were first published in *Poetry Wales*. Others have appeared in *Akros, The Anglo-Welsh Review, Y Bangoriad, BBC Cymru, Clw, Escape* (Groningen), *Y Gragen, Mabon, Planet,* the anthologies *Poems '69, Poems '70, Poems '71, Poems '72* (Gwasg Gomer), *Second Aeon,* and *Transatlantic Review.* Some are also recorded on Side One of the Argo disc PLP 1156.

CONTENTS

CONTENTS — *continued*

MARWNAD

For
Waldo
open the door
of silence. Let words blow
down the world's winds. Let language soar
for him, and swift verbs flow,
who on their shore
chants no
more.

Wales
(for whom
his words like gales
of leaves streamed, a swept plume
of speech, spirit's pinions and flails)
glows with a wine's soft bloom
in their jewelled grails.
Death's room
pales,

lit
by light
their walls transmit
like living chrysolite.
And in the wine the pearl which, split,
reveals within its white
and precious pit
the bright
grit :

heart
of him,
grain and rampart
too of his strength of limb.
But diamond without counterpart
he cut for the pilgrim
Wales his lines chart
and hymn :
art.

PLACES

There's a spot in Bangor, between
the climb of the College park
and the old Bishop's Palace—
I could lead you there in the dark.
On the map of my mind the place
is a paving-stone with the mark

of a cross. It's vivid today—
the scruffy hedge, the sudden stilled
ring of a passer-by's footsteps,
the sun going in, the air chilled,
and overhearing someone say
' Gandhi has been killed '.

EXPLANATORY NOTE

For some of us, you see,
Wales is another word for peace.
The changing of the guard
is not our national frontispiece.
We like our castles ruined.
Mountains green as the verdigris

overlaying old armour
are our image—in millpond lakes.
Wales is a word for life
without kings and lords, and the cakes
of living expertly sliced
into great wedges, slender flakes.

Wales is two languages,
not one : and both of them invoke
a ritual dragon
trampling a meadow green as oak
in one half ; but the other
white as Gandhi's cloak.

1944

The monasteries on the eve
of dissolution must have been
like Bangor then—caverns of cold,
rarely a movement to be seen
in cloisters, stairways, quadrangles.
Stillness within. Outside, the spleen

of weather, world and war. It was
a fortress abbey, like the one
on Lérins ; or a Templar house
with last, depleted garrison—
disabled, old, keeping the Rule
while brethren met the Saracen.

Three-quarters empty, still it held
the living legends of two knights,
Sir Ifor and the glimpsed Sir John.
A lifetime's service of the rites
had left them, like old tapers, bent
but, in that year of darkness, lights.

CARDIFF

Passing the Arms Park, hearing
the sixty-odd thousand fling
their battle chants, bay uproar
for their game of ritual war—
like that lion-tongued Roman
crowd, no doubt, when sweating men
fought in the scorch of Nero's
eye ; passing, the dark thought rose
how, outside the stadium,
so many of these are dumb
for their country—who acclaim
its crowning in a mere game.

NOSWAITH DA

Descending through the perpetually
poised waves and unbreaking foam
of the blackthorn, through hedgerows
dense as Keble Martin's *Flora*
with primrose, violet, red
campion and greater stitchwort,
I am aware of the high-stalked
white-flowered hemlock everywhere,
enough to put the village
underground. But it's Athens
the word calls up, and that evening
in 399 when the sloe-dark
shadows grew long on the swept
and sun-gold floor, and the weeping
messenger came with the cup.

EDINBURGH

i D. Myrddin Lloyd

' High up there the Gododdin
was first sung '—he stabbed a thin
index towards the castle.
Where we drove I couldn't tell—
that Myrddin's caer, Corstorphine,
as it turned out. But the lean
words stirred : Men went to Catraeth,
and I saw three hundred lithe
Welsh warriors thundering
down the granite, heard the ring
of blade on boss, on armour
stone-blue in shadow but more
bright than ice-fall in sunlight.
So on that September night
of the Festival, other
librettos were chanted there
than those bouqueted by bourgeois
art : Aneirin's gold-torqued joie
de vivre, grief, for heroes
wreathed and robed in the blood's rose.

CYWYDD I LANSTEFFAN

Language, work in Llansteffan's
praise. Praise the long ostrich fans
of the plumed sea winnowing
the two bays, the peacock wing
of the tide folded towards
the sunset. The castle wards
burst like a spread stone flower
on the hill-top, whose slopes wear
the verdigris-green village
forged by men of the Iron Age.
The hamlet of the seven
who rode to Agincourt when
the trumpet crowed nests neatly
below in the castle's lee,
feathered with owl and heron,
lichened slates mossed firmly on—
tight lids to the centuries'
kettles of fish. Among trees,
menhirs, fox-coloured bracken
dense over barrow and den
and set, our badger-lustrous
black and white, committed house.

TRAETH LLANSTEFFAN

Walking along the washed
skin of the world, under the high
ocean of the evening
heavens, only the insistent sigh
of the respiring
sea to be heard. The scoured rocks dry,

sculptured and matt, ice-blue
and Tyrian, acid as inks.
The promontory,
silhouetted, bulks like a sphinx
over the orient Tywi,
and the sun sinks.

COLOUR PRINT

All this magnificence
is not the strewn hall of the minotaur,
nor the rose-granite fall
of architraves that sunned an emperor ;
it is the panoply
of one serene frieze of Llansteffan shore,

sandstone outcropping in
imperial geology, with pale
blue inter-strata poised
among the purple, packed with mingled shale.
The figure resting there
is me, a cipher introduced for scale.

MAP READING

Look north if you like :
Eryri, water, Kirkcudbright,
the fingers of the Arctic sun
feeling out gold on the white
plains of the pole's Klondyke.

Look south even more :
Cardiff, the Bridge, and beyond
the Summer Country, Europe
shimmering up from the pond
of the Manche like a solar shore.

The west is all right :
the sea, the Republic, the crash
and spin of the ocean, furlongs
of light ; only then bulks the brash
American shore, and the night.

Best avoid the east :
below the Dyke it's getting dark
in the tangled, litter-blown
Greater London park
of Britain, deceased.

VIEW FROM LLANSTEFFAN

Stand on this rock.
Look over there, south by south-east.
There the *Paul of Hamburg* slid
down to the everlasting feast
of cockles and mussels,
the waves' yeast

and the storm's kitchen.
Now enswathed in the watered skeins
of long Cefn Sidan,
fitted forever to the grains
of the saffron sands,
the hulk remains

forfeit to Wales.
It came in peace, but the bay's jaw
bit it—like a flurried bird
pulled under for the old pike's maw.
Beware, then, you who want to come
and play at war.

AGINCOURT

Seven of the Welsh archers
whose arrows eclipsed the sun
in icy susurrations
when Agincourt was done
had gone there from Llansteffan.
When that day's death was won

if any of them lived
I wonder what they thought.
I live in Llansteffan
and I know Agincourt—
the bonemeal verdant meadows
over which they fought :

green places, both of them now,
but then, in 1415,
at Agincourt the blood
clotted the buttercups' sheen
and the earth was disembowelled
where stakes and hooves had been.

And far off, in Llansteffan,
castle, village and shore
flowered in the marigold sun.
Did those seven men explore
the contrast of this peace
with another English war ?

WATERLOO

Waterloo ? We went once.
There were several hours to fill
before we caught the boat.
A pyramidal, man-made hill
climbs greenly where the prince
of Orange took his final spill.

I didn't know before
that any Dutch were near the place.
I'd always thought it was
just French and Prussians face to face—
and the English of course,
that other violent race.

All have their cenotaphs
praising the field on which they bled,
but wheat—like the grand army
accoutred, bright and high of head—
is their true memorial,
dunged by forty-thousand dead.

China Wellington boots,
Napoleons, sell briskly here.
What Waterloo was for
the diorama makes quite clear—
the royal Belgian
tourist industry, it would appear.

SHALOM

Amnon, Gideon, Shimon,
where are you now ?
Practising precision ?
I taught you how.

Joel, Giora, David,
what are you at ?
Taking the line's full sweep ?
I taught you that.

Daniel, Ilan, Elisha,
what is your task ?
Interrogation ?
I taught you to ask.

Rachel, Nourith, Yael,
what do you do ?
Reject the sentimental ?
I taught that too.

O children of Israel,
my pupils once
in a Dutch oasis,
genius and dunce,

what have I taught you,
what will grow next
from those tranquil mornings
at work on a text ?

But I send my greeting ;
for what I heard
grow through those lines
was this green word.

THAT WINTER

I remember that winter, 'sixty-three,
when all Europe froze ;
and we in the middle—as far from Wales
as from the great white rose
of storm-wrapped Warsaw, thickly petalled
in the same whorled snows.

There, on the frontier, the forest burned
in a steel white cold,
and Juffrouw Sissingh drove Amsterdamwards—
as soon as the ice would hold—
over the Zuider Zee, a glass Ukraine.
The planet seemed old—

old and white and dead, like another moon.
One wondered now and then
(saying nothing) whether the polar pelt
was inching south again,
to stifle in the rug of its bear-hug
the warm world of men.

Within a day's drive out of Paris
grey wolves were seen—
and photographed : lithe images of death,
hungry, keen-eyed, lean.
Would sun-warmth ever again turn them back,
would grass show green ?

So we drove down the dead length of Europe—
white Belgium, France,
black trees, myopic ice, no birds, grey skies,
a world of sculptured trance ;
up, over the alps, and down—to meet
mimosa in Provence.

WALES TO THE NETHERLANDS

Just as cartography
your notion that, on the North Sea,
there floats an island called
England, wholly water-walled,
is quite mistaken.
This misconception, taken
to its logical end
on our side, should make us send
letters across that sea
to you in ' Groningen, Germany '.
But such cosmography
you find annoying ? So do we.
That English isle exists
only in your geography's mists.

Reach once more for the map :
that island in the water's lap
is Britain, and three lands
stretch north, west, south, within its sands.
Sharing the German plain,
you are not Germany. Abstain
then, we would ask you now,
from your tendency to endow
the innocent North Sea
with a Greater English Reich we
and no one wants to see.

SNAPSHOT

Sophia Gardens offer
better dahlias by far.

The quondam Kaiser's flower-garden :
Elwyn and I taking the sun,
myself reviewing royals
through glinting lenses ground in Wales.

What was he like, that old bandit
Wilhelm, who contrived to sit
out thirty years in this pastoral
patch of Holland, after all
his crimes ? This half-English Prussian
junker whom both races shun—
perhaps because he embodied
the worst of both, in style and deed ?
The curious humourlessness
about titles and fancy-dress
for instance : that coal-bucket
on his head, he seemed to get
unfathomable pleasure
from violence beyond all cure.
The double-bed sized mantle—
Roman ? Freudian ? who can tell.
Then *highness, majesty, all-highest*—
that need to wear a woollen vest
of words to warm and insulate
the thin blood from the human state.

At Wilhelm's little castle
here at Doorn today they sell
a tour of the imperial
loot. It's curious how real
estate accompanies reckless
malefactors of this class
into exile : mere train robbers
seem naive as the three bears.
Not to be parted from their porridge
is an old royal privilege.
Centuries of self-seeking
go to make a successful king—
through lack of long tradition
the common thief's undone.

Did he learn anything, this Wilhelm ?
A shoe-tree trying to be an elm
is still the last impression
mirrored in the glossy run
of postcards sold as souvenirs :
he learnt nothing from the years.

And that is why, old scoundrel,
I feel for you now, and tell
your empty tale : it's the human
condition—poor strutting man,
you, I, most of us, ending
implacably pretending.

Behind the waxed moustaches
what anguish, what ashes.

INVOLVEMENT

In Wenceslas Square
an old man weeps.
Here in Wales
my numbed hand wipes

his streaming tears.
Small countries know
that Acts of Union
are nothing new.

We are all one country.
This one feels
the heart's hot flush
when that one falls.

There is one oppressor :
a state of mind
crude as armies
no law can mend.

The armour here
in which it rides ?
Tanks of tourists
thud the roads.

The quiet casualties
die without flowers—
villages, visions,
life's doused flares.

And what are the values,
where these once stood,

the occupiers
bring instead ?

Cake and circuses—
profits of tours,
and a pantomime
in Caernarfon towers.

Adapt Yourselves
is Prague's cold hope.
How many here
jump through the hoop

like circus dogs,
proud of the ease
with which they learn
to compromise ?

The brash ringmasters
flutter their whips
in the greasy capitals.
One man weeps,

but how many caper
and suit their tone
to London's, Moscow's,
Washington's tune ?

In Wenceslas Square
an old man's eyes
melt for his fatherland
and us.

DATES

1301
In Caernarfon keep
the title draped round Edward's son,
a player prince, the first of the heap.
Where Llywelyn, known to none,
sleeps his last sleep
the green weeds run.

1404
and Glyn Dŵr treats
with pope and French ambassador.
Wales is in Europe, and its streets
lead Londonwards no more.
English Henry beats
at the door.

1535
and Holbein's king,
Henry the hog-smooth, still alive—
gnawing at Rome like a capon wing,
and once again about to wive :
with Wales. The ring—
an iron gyve.

1649
Colonel John Jones
and Thomas Wogan undersign
the first axe swung at Europe's thrones.
But Charles's son will soon refine
such bold Welsh bones
and blood to brine.

And then today,
with nothing learned,
nothing forgotten. Still the play
climbs to the boards, all unconcerned
that mummery has had its day.
Who less aware time turned
than they ?

MARSEILLAISE

There's always one thing to be said
For France : it's a republic. Once we stopped
in Colombey-les-Deux-Eglises
(at the top of his time) and, passing, dropped
into the church—resonant, dark
as an antique 'cello : a good deal topped

with gilt and lace and candle-wax
in the old, comfortable way. Stark as stocks
the pews, with their cards—*Général
et Madame de Gaulle* among them ; the knocks
of sabots pewtering the wood.
No vulgar plush carnationed royal box.

ORANGES AND LEMONS

Angharad and I were walking
in Ommen forest one day
when this great car rocked gently round
the bend, on the sandy way
through the woods. The orange pennon
rose and sank serenely, gay

as a flag on a child's sand-castle.
At the front a chauffeur sat ;
some distance behind, Mevrouw—
a presence, rather than fat
one might say ; smiling beneath
waved hair and a dowdy hat.

Juliana van Oranje-
Nassau, mother of the State :
Angharad recognised the face
from the classroom State portrait.
They waved. I nodded to a good
woman, but turned to the gate.

DIRECTIONS FOR VISITORS

If you want to see Wales,
measure the long isosceles
of Snowdon with your feet ;
fly your heart through the dappled trees
of calm Cwm Cynfal ; dip
your finger-tips into the lees

of the old religion
at Holywell—and see the new
at pink Llantrisant mint.
Ascend the sacred avenue
of Strata Florida :
beyond the transept seek the yew,

the flame of evergreen
that streams up from dead Dafydd's bones,
and know that there, under
the sheep-cropped turf and tumbled stones,
are clenched the corded roots
stronger than new pence or old thrones.

DOCUMENTARY

1

Swansea, 8th May, 1971 :
a Saturday, about tea-time.
Before the Brangwyn Hall a lake
of people, young and old, sitting.
It might be a Quaker meeting,
a pool of quiet in the sun,
or an open-air convention,
a rest on a charity walk.
But they are sitting on the road,
sitting round a blue police-van
islanded
in their midst with its tyres let down.
It contains perhaps six people
arbitrarily arrested.
Time passes. A chief policeman
comes, threatens in the wrong language
the curious charge of assault.
Time passes. People carefully
climb in and out, to stretch their legs,
buy sandwiches. And time passes.
The sun beams down on the calm lake,
on the hundreds, on the blue van.

2

There is movement
upon the shores.
The policemen
seem to thicken.
The sun goes in.

Walkers, talkers
come and sit down.
The lake receives
them in, extends
its still surface.
Others come and
place themselves at
the brim, parents,
professors, a
man on crutches,
ministers of
the religion
of gentleness
but justice too.
Vans begin to
arrive, one or
two containing
dogs, though these were
in fact not used.

3

Some of the vans are blue,
others are white. The first
reverses to the brim.
It is square, metallic,
like a mobile oven.
The doors are thrown open.
Out of the lake is flung a long rope of singing—
the hymnody of the great foursquare chapels,
which bound the clop and clatter of dragoons,
plaiting the nerves into the song's strong cable
to which they hold as the victims are selected.

Swiftly, efficiently,
the police start their work.
Like reapers entering
the calm wheat's golden song,
they try to cut their swathe.
Into the vacant space
a group of older men
advance : distinguished names
are offered. Utterly
they are refused. Only
the young will serve. The
law is selective. Edicts
have clearly been issued.
With hindsight now we see
Black Hatred et cetera
to be the intended
official line, rather
hard to sustain with group
arrests of ministers
of the gospel of love—
unless it is implied
that they are charlatans.
And even this is tried.
So van replaces van,
the harvest is swung in,
and the harvest song soars.

4

Nothing has been achieved. The lake
flows in and fills the cut channel.
The police are withdrawn. They form
in two ranks some distance away,
are clearly being instructed.

The last van,
large and white,
is backed in,
inched towards
the lake's brim.

Along / each side
two files / in black
advance. / They wade
into / the lake,
straight in, / treading
water, / thrusting
forwards / towards
the first / blue van.
Shrieks, screams / of girls.
Limp forms / are passed
out of / the lake,
laid on / the bank
gently. / They weep.

Appalled bystanders, on an evening stroll,
rush forward incredulous to the edge.
Moch, they shout, Pigs. But do pigs do such things
to their own kind ? A young man seated there
sternly forbids the shouting of abuse,
restarts the singing. Now the great hymns roll
in breakers of polyphony, engulf
the thrusting, crushing tramplers of the peace.
Order is kept by the young, and solfa.
Violence in the uniform of law
succeeds, of course, because it counts upon
assumptions of the victim's reverence
for law. Not all the provocation
of judges and police can even now
kick this non-violence to retaliate.

The violence succeeds. The two black lines
straddle the dense canticle of the lake,
reach the first van, hustle its prisoners
across. The lake rises and pours into

two   streams
which   sweep
down   round
the   van's
white   sides
and   front.
They   sit.

        The   police   panic.
They   throw   lunge   thrust
      drag   push   scatter.
A   sergeant   runs   amok
      into   bystanders, middle-
aged   women,   who   stagger
      before   his   rush.
One's   instinct   is   to
      call   a   policeman.
The   full   enormity   is
      that   policemen   are
now   beyond   all   call.

        The van revvs up,
swerves this way,
           turns that,
feints wildly,
          swerves again
      improbably,
        and
           escapes
            at
              speed.

Miraculously, no one is run down
fatally though a doctor attends one
young woman stretched out on the road.

5

The violence has succeeded, as it
often does at the time. Its failure is
therefore assured. A cause which can make
the full embattled violence of the
establishment expose itself has won.
The rituals remain, no doubt—the fines
to be paid, or not paid, as the case may be.
The usual sententious or malicious
bids from benches for the headlines will occur
for a while. But the paradox of peace
kept by the public, violence performed
by the police, is writing on the wall.
Some policemen, like some magistrates,
begin to hang back. Cracks are appearing
in the wall itself. Somewhere high up
behind it, in a ministerial
suite, the compromise is being worked out.
It is the wise politician who is
not made the scapegoat for his predecessors'
misjudgements. That last careering van
is already a bandwagon on which
many are wisely preparing to jump.

6

The prisoners will be released at once,
two of them without charges. Yet for this
the police have put the public at risk,
trampled on women, on their own image,
arrested forty citizens for sitting still,
discredited the law and the law's officers,
the peaked caps and the silver horsehair wigs
under which such violent notions beat.

The police retire to the central lawn
around the union jack. Certain violent
civilians in suits and short haircuts
are now revealed as plain-clothes men.
All look rather pink and flustered, big boys
who will be boys, but are uneasily aware
that after all this was not the Springboks,
that things have been done today about which
implacable questions will be levelled.

For a week the London media
filibuster about demonstrations
in Washington, Sweden and Moscow :
injustice is a regrettable
well-known foreign phenomenon.

With the cameras of language
the antipoem must be shot,
the precise documentary
of the inexorable word.

THE JUDGE'S TALE

I am not as you,
a citizen, a cipher on the roll.
I am privileged—few,
indeed, more so. For me your church bells toll,

your police adjust
their shoulders, faces, and their traffic rules.
When I enter you must
stand up. My rabbit fur and robe of gules

set me apart, my wig
makes me remote from you. Here I am king.
This royal fig
instructs, reminds you there is no such thing

as the people's courts.
Construct your common justice if you can,
but in your thoughts.
Law is a lord, not a common man.

LUNCH BREAK

Here at Aust, where the Bridge springs
to its feet by the spinnings
of the Severn, the cliff's drop,
long ago Austin bishop
of Canterbury remained
seated. The Welsh prelates, pained
at his barbarity, blew
out their curled beards and withdrew
across the water to Wales
and civilisation. Gales
of commination billowed
acridly down the next wide
centuries. Austin's Roman
civility, dulled by men
of that Teutonic kingdom
of the south, worn thin, brought doom
here on his nunciature :
his manners marred the future.

Life gave him a long Lent's chance
to purge out his arrogance,
but most don't. They still ride up
from those steppes, dazed by the cup
of their pride, and think that that
will serve them here. You ask at
whom I raise my fingertip ?
Instances, you ask ? Just dip
your hand and see which you pull
out. Judges, for example.

JUDGMENT DAY

Who are these lords
in bogus hair and hunting pink
who sit like totems
enthroned up there on the brink
of illusion
and reality, and think

that all the world's
their court ? Secular prelates ?
Staffordshire dogs
on the mantlepiece of fate's
front room ? Keepers
of the pillories of states ?

Woe unto you,
lords justices, beyond both
good and evil—
robed in your law's runes, but loath
to learn the lessons
of the waking spirit's growth.

Woe unto you
whose ancient insolence assails
conscience and youth.
Behold, the august and sacred scales
tremble and tip.
Be sentenced now yourselves, from Wales.

PUBLIC GALLERY

Your worships (as they say), with all respect
you're not what I had been led to expect.

I sit and observe you over my glasses.
Conduct like this would not do in my classes.

Pert or insolent, mute, uncritical,
no Welsh at all, and English pitiful—

how did you get there ? Whose nomination ?
What conceivable qualification ?

The usual, no doubt. Bourgeois ambition,
Freemasonry, party composition.

You are the British predilection
for amateurism in local section.

Scarcely surprising that things have gone wrong.
We have been absent from our courts too long

(for they are our courts)—the critical,
the articulate, the professional.

Compare the quality of the defendants
with that of justice's blind attendants.

Appalled, I watch the alienation
of the finest minds of a generation.

Your law, your courts, your police, will fall to them.
It is yourselves that your words condemn.

Expect the scourging of the Furies
when these become your judges, juries.

But I am wrong. They are compassionate
and understand what brought you to this state.

As they look down upon you from their places
there in the dock, pity moves their faces.

They contemplate, from the elevation
you force them to, the wreckage of a nation.

AFTER GOETHE

Uber allen Gipfeln | Ist Ruh'

Over all the mountain tops is peace,
    and the October sea
pastures calmly, its innocent fleece
    of foam skeined on the sand.
The land relaxes, stretched at poised ease

like a coloured plaster contour map,
    pristine and fresh painted.
All is clear and clean—the overlap
    of vegetation on
each modelled peak, moulded river-gap,

defined and tactile. After the stealth
    of last night's salt of frost,
cottage gardens glow with a crisp wealth
    of red-gold roses. Wales
seems a landscape shimmering with health.

But here and there, in a fluted cirque
    of the mountains, or lodged
in some river valley's florid quirk,
    note the angry pustules,
hectic red : judges and courts at work.

ANEIRIN SPEAKS

Beirdd byd barnant wŷr o galon

The poets of the people
will judge who are the men of courage.
Note that the poets will judge :
not the mister justices, police,
the lawyers and magistrates,
the creaking computers of the law.
For language is not of them :
it belongs to poets and people.

The poets of the people
will judge who are the men of courage—
and the women too. So I
with wife, with sister-in-law, son, all
arrested within eight days
for the cause of the language, commend
them to the people's poets,
to the people, to men of courage.

ANTHEM FOR DOOMED YOUTH

Abertawe, 22 Tachwedd 1971

My hope is on what is to come.
I turn in anguish from the servile, dumb

present—from an indifferent people, shut
to justice, crouching in the heart's dark hut.

I turn to the future, to a Wales hung
with the names, like garlands, of today's young.

Outside the court the three stood in the sun,
poised, at ease, in the soft chrysanthemum

light of Swansea, the bitter city. They
alone knew freedom on that icy day.

Policemen, advocates, recognised in those
the radiance of the uncorrupted rose

glowing above their court well's mantled scum.
Even the judge, that perched geranium,

saw it ; and traded on it—to retail,
after the verdict, his unheard of bail,

honouring their integrity's claim
which he would deny when sentence came.

O unjust judge, mere expert in the sleight
of hand of law, do you sleep at night ?

Be sure your victims sleep sounder than you
in the bitter place you condemned them to.

And you, Mr Secretary of State,
setter up of committees, what fate

have the history books in store for you,
who can watch while the young are spitted through ?

who can wait on a touring troupe's report
while conscience is crucified in court ?

My rhyme tolls for you all, beats its slow drum.
My hope is on what is to come.

PASSION 72

9 Chwefror 1972

' They arrested him
and led him away '.
How often have I
heard newscasters say
in the past twelve-month
the same momentous
words of Luke. The police
are always with us,
Roman, Dyfed-Powys,
and the Passion
unfolds before us
in unchanging fashion.

The unjust trial scene
endlessly recurs :
Socrates bears his,
Portia stages hers.
It moves to Moscow,
Ulster ; now to Wales—
at Mold and Swansea
the thorns and nails.
By sweating judges
and magistrates, mazed
by sacred Caesar,
the crosses are raised.

For Pilate abides
too, bewigged or bald,
in pink, or pin-stripe
suit today, and called
my lord, your worship.
A peppercorn still
on the judgment seat,
he's ground in the mill
of the police, the scribe
and the pharisee,
washes his hands of
justice, goes to tea.

What can it be like,
though, to draw their breath,
grow towards old age
and sentence of death
with such a conscience ?
To brood on the fact
that Pilate's name
and his unjust act
endure to this day ?
To know their wages
the execration
of the ages ?

ARCHETYPES

Lord Caiaphas, high priest
of this mumbo jumbo,
flunkey surrounded, policed :
rip your black robe, gold laced,
tear your perwigged hair,
and stamp your lord high foot
on justice prostrate there.

Sir Pontius, ex-colonel,
Mr Justice Pilate—
urbane epitome
of alien law and state :
used to settling natives
in undeveloped lands,
he passes savage sentence
and washes his hands.

Herod, called king, poor thing,
but merely Pilate's clerk,
rootless deracinate—
become a dog to bark
at his master's bidding ;
to snap from a manger
no honest man covets.
To justice, a stranger.

And the defendant : God.
And down the ages God
in the men and women
stumbling the track he trod,
far off, imperfectly,
derided, bruised, but lit
by justice in the heart,
that candles time's dark pit.

GHOSTS

Pilate, Herod, Caiaphas,
when their souls were asked of them,
could not pass from life in peace.
Not for them the requ em
Aprilling poor sinners' souls.
Endless night's insomnia
while unwinking time unrolls
they condemned themselves to bear.

Still they haunt the Judgment Seat,
icing with their own despair
brains that lock beneath the wigs,
eyes that stare down from the bench
not at citizens but pigs,
baboons fantasy has bred.
Still more chilling, Judas too
now has risen from the dead.

JOHN ROBERTS, TRAWSFYNYDD

Today in Rome
under the thrush-egg blue of the dome
of Peter, Paul
enthroned, tiaraed, will hallow all
your deeds, and raise
you to the world's altars and heaven's blaze.

It's a long way
in time and space from that winter day
at Tyburn tree ;
further still from Rhiwgoch, from the scree
above the cwm
of abbatial Cymer's holy room.

From Paris too,
and Compostella, which both knew you ;
far from and yet
most near to Gellilydan, where we met
in the snow's smirch
to honour you in the candled church.

What I recall
years after, most vividly of all,
is on a bus
back to Blaenau, in a bulb's nimbus
your reliquary,
under its veil, bouncing on my knee.

Today in Wales
far from the Fisherman and the sails
of mitres, copes
spread now to the huge wind of your hopes,
I think of you
drawn from a parish where I lived too.
I on that day
was even closer to you than they.

ST JOHN JONES

What's in a name? Some twenty
thousand people probably,
who—though the intoning
Roman glottis could not ring
the unItalian J—
answer to it every day.
Your sainting thus epitomised
the common Welshman canonised—
you in our loaf the leaven.

Is it far from Clynnog to heaven?
I think of you strolling in that
eternal Wales, a cartwheel hat
perched on your head above the brown
tucked-up old Franciscan gown,
George Herbert, Ann Griffiths there,
and the immortal air
sun-shafted with all your talk
on that green walk.

JOHN KEMBLE, 1679—1970

Today you are a saint,
invocable, laid open to
votive candles, novenas ;
a principal now in the
theatre of God, your name
in the dramatis personae
of the eternal passion play.
I think of you, a little dazed
by the sudden spotlights
after the three quiet centuries,
as one who might be saying ' How
comes an old priest of my age
to find himself on this bright stage ?
What I remember, gentle
old man, is how you smoked
one final, wreathing pipe and
sipped a parting cup of sack,
savouring life and Hereford
until the hangman spoke the word.

ACCLAMATION

Mawr ac ardderchog fyddai y rhain yn eich chwedl,
Gymry, pe baech chwi'n genedl.

—Waldo Williams
' Wedi'r Canrifoedd Mudan '

I

1970. October twenty-fifth. Rome.
A Welsh eye in the dome,
you look from Michelangelo's height
    down to the plain of light
below—the vast and distant chessboard floor,
    like the raised marble shore
of the world's immense Gennesaret,
    where a great crowd is set
today, the gospel multitudes still led
    by the heart's golden thread.
Through the tide of faces, wave on wave,
    advancing up the nave—
triumphal avenue of Christendom—
    the twelve disciples come,
miraculously multiplied like loaves
    and fishes. The veined mauves
and scarlets of the blood that they must shed
    if need be, martyr red,
mantle the bishops—reminder to them
    of the stake's diadem
and the colour of gibbet and block.
    Then, following his flock
and leaning on his staff, the last of all,
    comes the chief shepherd, Paul.

A column of calm crimson, they flow
    up the basilica's slow
length, like red in a thermometer :
    the living blood of Peter.

                    2
    Of course you realise
    that this was seen through the eyes
    of the imagination
    only. Though the nation
    was honoured at the heart
    of Christendom, played a part
    on the stage of history,
    mere clippings of the story
    were seen and heard in Wales.
    Its significance pales
    to nothing when compared
    to some ten-times re-aired
    royal irrelevance,
    or the breath-taking chance
    of beholding in reflection
    an American election.

    This was about true choice.
    This was about the voice
    of conscience, about man
    immortal in his span ;
    about the acclamation
    of courage in a nation.
    It was, no doubt, not a patch
    on a football match.
    But, to be frank, who needier
    of a mass than the media ?

And so the mass begins, the poetry
of God. It is, of course, a symmetry
of word, sound, colour, perfume, movement, stone.
God is not worshipped by the word alone,
but every art combines in creation
of liturgy, the communication
of God and his assembled people :
words can be wagging bells in a steeple,
archaic noise. Liturgy re-enacts
moments of a life of radiant acts
as well as words—entry, offering, kiss,
washing, blessing, and the great Do This
of the upper room. The dense fragrance
of lilies of the field, blue incense
smoke, ascending like a visible prayer,
can make a gospel of the empty air—
recall the vase of perfume she poured
over his feet, and thus recall the Lord
of the body, spirit and senses too.
The clothes we wear are the cut and hue
of the dusty world of fashion, trade,
custom and change. When they are overlaid
with the seamless garment of Christ, calm white
the eye is hushed towards the world of light.
In a red vestment, like those of today,
colour can speak of the opened way
to liberation through the Red Sea's flood,
the Spirit's tongues of fire, the martyr's blood.
Man in the gospels touches, tastes and scents,
sees and hears the God who made each sense.

In liturgy the same God re-appears
in signs to touch man's tongue and eyes and ears,
so that the gospel moves again. Today's
is re-enacted to the martyrs' praise.

4

It was a Quaker who first planted
the laurels of their praise in poetry.
Waldo, prince of poets, chanted

their service, rang their bells in his steeple.
He—of that gentle Society of Friends,
another persecuted people—

felt them as friends, as a master-band
binding Wales and heaven in one society :
God their father, and their fatherland.

He too had suffered, and his name is warm
in Wales for a kind of martyrdom
for conscience, for refusing to conform.

' Great in your annals their acclamation,
Welshmen (he sang) were you a nation '.
Today they mount to this assignation

with history, are raised to the altars.
These six sons of Wales who walked in the furnace
of Nebuchadnezzar, with the psalters

of life in their hands, are our seraphim :
today they bring the world's honour to Wales.
And so today, with them, I sing of him—

Waldo, prifardd, archpoet, harbinger
of this day, prophetic voice of Wales ;
in him honour saints and song and singer.

5
The litanies begin.
Who are these in white robes,
whose spirits fill the dome ?
They are the kith and kin
of the six to be named
today, drawn from their home
in the calendar, the map
of Wales, the dedications
of ancient churches poised
in circular enclosures,
toothed with Ogham stones and chipped
dog-Latin inscriptions ;
set on the tops of mountains,
lost in long-grassed meadows,
crumbling on the foreshores
of the perpetually
praying, Celtic sea.
David of Menevia,
dove on his shoulder ;
Dyfrig, and Patrick
apostle of Ireland,
Illtyd, and Cadog the wise ;
the saints of the islands—
Iestyn, Samson, Dwynwen,
Cybi the tawny
and Seiriol the fair ;

Winefride of the well
of sweet water ; Melangell
of the hunted hare ;
the stern bishops and abbots,
Beuno, Teilo, Padarn,
Asaff, and Deiniol the blessed.
And there, radiant among
the patriarchal beards,
squat mitres, glittering
chasubles, behold the young
George Herbert in his country
parson's cloth, and gentle Ann
of Dolwar, nightingale of Christ.
So, as the litanies
rise and fall in the vast
cave of the basilica,
the saints of Wales draw near—
a cloud of witnesses
thronging the middle air.

6

And now the eternal mystery
of holiness stops short for history.
Before the enthroned Roman Pontiff,
in the great silence, distant Cardiff
speaks on the tongue of a bishop of Wales.
To Christendom's ear his voice unveils
the martyrs' virtues in magnificence
of Welsh. Over the listening, incense-
laden air the waves of language ride,
like a chiselled inscription. Then take pride,
Welshmen, that in the august, unbroken
hush of the dome's heart Welsh has been spoken.

7

What do they know or care at home
about what's happening in Rome
today ? It's Sunday, day of rest,
set apart by most to digest
a banquet of English crime.
The week's police-court pantomime,
re-staged, cuts its pathetic capers
libretto'd by the Sunday papers.
This in fact is that vaunted, great
international culture in full spate
in market-conditioned Wales—
which, feet on mantlepiece, regales
itself with Eden's sad scrub-apples.
Three-quarters empty churches, chapels,
moulder among the bingo halls.
This is one Wales. Within its walls
is warmth, compassion, life aflame.
But even those who bear the name
John Jones have never heard of him.
The name is mere parental whim—
no notion of the celebration
of the brave of their own nation.
John Jones, John Penry, Richard Gwyn
are not the names their lives deal in,
not the names the media promote.
Names of demagogues they could quote
by the dozen—criminals, stars,
politicians, princelings, the czars
of America, Russia, Spain ;
London's provincial and inane
dramatis personae—masters
of the columnists, newscasters.

The media and education,
that process of alienation,
have made them experts in the vast
detritus of the world : the past
and present of their own world strange
as Cantre'r Gwaelod's unknown range.

8

Hebrews, eleven. Paul
names the holy ones of old.
Today another Paul
names six new saints of Wales.
No man can open heaven :
they have been there all the time,
but naming them honours them,
their names, their nation, their deeds.
The oldest voice of Europe,
Peter's, who near this place—
in the Neronian circus—
was crucified upside down ;
whose bones lie deep below
the paved plain of this floor,
upon the lost green contour
of the buried Vatican hill ;
whose monument this is—
the Galilee fisherman's hut
raised to the power of n
and the greater glory of God :
the voice of Peter, that speaks
through nineteen centuries,
now falls on the quiet air—
calmly, firmly, proclaims
six commonplace Welsh names.

9

Richard Gwyn, teacher. Born at Llanidloes.
Done to death in the Beast Market, Wrexham.
Wales could do worse than listen to his voice.

Martyrs' blood grows
wherever sown.
The poor schoolmaster
comes into his own—
in Flint where he taught
a school has grown.
In Wrexham where he bled
bishops have their throne.
The rock rejected
is the cornerstone.

John Jones, Franciscan friar, of Clynnog Fawr.
Young and serene, on London's stony ground
his spirit smiled into blood-red flower.

A man lived in Assisi
gentle as light ;
the sun was his brother,
his sister, night.

A man lived in Clynnog,
green place of grace ;
Assisi called him
across time and space.

John of Clynnog followed
to his heart's last breath ;
Saint Francis his brother,
his sister, death.

John Roberts, monk of Saint Benedict.
Born at Trawsfynydd. At Tyburn tree
his heart unleaved, and the long flames licked.

Over Trawsfynydd
the iced wind sweeps ;
on Rhiwgoch stones
the white rain weeps.

By the rain sifted,
by the wind shorn,
from stern Trawsfynydd
a saint is born.

Philip Evans, Jesuit, Monmouth born ;
John Lloyd, secular, of Brecon. They died
together : John must first watch Philip torn.

Boxed in Cardiff Castle
in the black Black Tower,
two candles waiting
for the flame's hour.

They were playing tennis
when the sentence came ;
they heard it serenely
and finished their game.

That night they played the harp
in Cardiff's Black Tower
in the morning the candles
burst into flower.

David Lewis of Abergavenny,
Jesuit. Called father of the poor :
one of the few who loved the many.

    For thirty years he loved them,
      in faith and hope.
    It was an old man
      they took for the rope.

    The hacked limbs of the others
      fed the fire's maw.
    When David Lewis hung,
      the crowd would have no more.

    Alone of them all, he lies
      in Wales, in Usk.
    Gaze over the waving wheat
      sprung from that husk.

10

These are the named ones, but I shall name
as well those Protestant consciences
of Wales who chose the scaffold and the flame :

Rawlins White, poor Cardiff fisherman ;
William Nichol of Haverfordwest ;
John Penry of Llangamarch, Puritan ;

the Anglican Robert Ferrar, his last breath
drawn in Carmarthen. As I cross Nott Square
I make my act of sorrow for each death.

O religion of love and gentleness,
its emblem the non-violent crucifix :
how was Calvary corrupted to this ?

—that Christians butcher Christians, and defraud
their maker of his image in all men,
and from the cross and ploughshare beat a sword.

Acclamation and reparation lie
at the heart of this day, and that is why
all Wales, not just one part, meets in the eye

of Peter and the world. They arm us,
the martyrs past and present, for today,
and for today's *Te deum laudamus*.

II

What is martyrdom ? Non-compromise.
Extremism when extremes are forced.
Resistance to the juggernaut that tries

to flatten all beneath the monstrous wheels
that trundle the gross idol of the State.
Martyrdom is the digging in of heels,

whatever the cost, at the point where most
will drag their heels and climb back on the fence.
Martyrs are always few, the innermost

élite of a nation, called to be brave
at the crossroads of human dignity,
where the crowds and the demagogues rave.

So martyrs abide, like the English gaols
that held them, then and now. I shall not name
today's—young men, young women, of Wales

who go singing to the prisons for love
of things invisible, like those of old,
resplendent in the wisdom of the dove.

12

Slowly the prelates leave :
cardinalatial scarlets blaze and weave
    with vivid magpie black
and white as the long tide flows slowly back.
    Violet and crimson file
down the long Champs Elysées of the aisle.
    Upon his litter, high
above the crowds, the Fisherman goes by,
    leaning to left and right,
imparting benediction to the tight-
    packed multitudes. The bells
of Rome boom, clash and chime, and in the wells
    of shadowed, fountained squares
the sudden distant tumult stirs and blares,
    flutters a Tiber quay
and fades away across the glittering sea.

13

And far across the sea, in Welsh churches,
now is the time for *Gloria in excelsis* :
in the thronged cathedrals of Cardiff and Wrexham,
where the dense candles blaze like banked flowers ;

in the white abbey of Caldey,
where Strata Florida, Tintern,
and Valle Crucis sing again :
in the choir of the Franciscan friars of Pantasaph,
brothers of Tudur Aled and Saint John of Clynnog ;
in the cloisters of the Benedictine dames of Talacre,
sisters of Saint John Roberts ;
in the grey walls of the Jesuits at Tremeirchion,
brethren of Saint Philip Evans, Saint David Lewis ;
in the Beast Market at Wrexham,
wet with the blood of Saint Richard Gwyn ;
in the holy places of Holywell and Penrhys,
where through the mute centuries
the faithful never ceased to come ;
in the thousand churches, old and new,
and in the corrugated-iron hall of Llansteffan—
best of all because lent in charity :
in all
let there be glory
for the martyrs and their story.

14

The canticle rises, drifts over Wales
with the high, plumed clouds swanning Llyn Gwynant.
A darkness like prehistory assembles
over the arched, dinosaur spine of Tryfan.
The day ends. Below the motorway,
Cardiff, Bridgend, Port Talbot, glitter into light
like a dressed fleet in tranquil anchorage.
On the long shores of Wales, the frayed cuffs
of the sea scuffle the sands' brown wrists.

The spinning waters weave rochets of foam
round rocks violet as bishops' soutanes.
Inexorably the tide ascends the beaches,
the western sea of the saints returning,
lustral, serene, rolling with benediction.

' Great in your annals would be their acclamation,
Welshmen, were you a nation '. Today they are
acclaimed. Wales, be worthy of your station.

*Commissioned by the Welsh Arts Council, and broadcast in a
production for radio by BBC Cymru on 24th February 1972.*

ANCESTORS

William Oliver maker
of winnowing machines, John Wood
labourer, in the fields of
the eighteenth century. You are good
forefathers for a man to have.
You might have understood

my making with words, my zest
for earth and spade. William Beere
tea merchant, savouring the joke.
And William Garlick, pioneer
of that name in Wales, who long
ago committed me here.

But of them all, the humble names
in the registers, I think of you
Nicholas Garlick, martyr,
and Derby Bridge your rendezvous,
in the armada year, with light.
You were an extremist too.

FOOTNOTE

To be frank, England
is a country that I just don't know.
I was born there, of course,
in London, some forty years ago ;
grew up, was schooled there,
in my fifteenth year was forced to go

to a factory there
to earn my bread. And then at eighteen
I was born again
in the granite and ultramarine
of Bangor, made free
at last of suburbia's pink patine.

That's England for me—
soliptical London, a stain
on the mind's old map ;
and today, what must be crossed to gain
Dover, Southampton,
and through them Belgium, Italy, Spain

and the world one knows,
familiar contexts of French and Dutch.
England is the lost
constriction of childhood, beyond touch
and relevance now.
One can't believe one has missed much.

AUGUST COUNTRY

That's what Wales was, for me
as a child : an Edward Thomas land
of holidays, the blood's tree
warm with nightingales ; the span of sand
a fortnight in the year's infinity.

What now, with thirty years gone ?
Wife and children, allegiance, degree,
long friendship to grasp upon ;
but still the lyric in the heart's tree,
and Traeth Llansteffan to stumble on.

Still August country, but now
august as its images candesce :
the old hulk history's prow
sinking at last in the firm sands' press,
and a dovecote built on the brain's bough.

IEUAN AP HYWEL SWRDWAL

Swrdwal, you are
our ancestor, the arch-poet
of those who write
in English, did they know it.

What was it like,
that Oxford of new gables,
honey-coloured walls,
in which you turned the tables?

Even the calm
Virgin, her griefs forgotten,
must have smiled to see
a literature begotten.

You sang for her,
threw the English your laughter.
I still hear it
five centuries after.

CISTERCIANS

Albalanda, Hendy Gwyn
ar Dâf, Whitland : names wherein
the holy white of that way
is fixed forever. Doomsday
will dazzle with serene light
streaming from the calm snow-white
sierras of all abbeys
of Citeaux. Hives of the bees
of Bernard, within your walls—
whether the sculptured snowfalls
of today, or the ruins
through Europe of all Christ's inns
raised by the white monks—in these
my mind lodges, finds heartsease,
glimpsing through each portico
the lyric rose in the snow.
Samson of Caldey, afloat
on your abbey's silver moat ;
Aelred, abbot of Rievaulx :
I seek the secret you know—
the unflawed oneness of song
you lived, heart and word's diphthong :
the lyric, snow fresh, sun warm,
flowering in the nave of form.

HEROES

They are not much in my line ;
memorial meetings and such.
If I knew them, they live on
in my own adrenalin's clutch.
For D.J. and J.C.P.
the heart's muscle needs no crutch.

For others, all I can say
is that once, years ago, I made
a journey to honour a man
whose name my boyhood had weighed—
Clemens August von Galen,
and the tombstone it overlaid.

Lion of Munster they called him
and I sought him out in his den,
winding into Germany—
Daniel country for me then,
language, land and people—
to the chancel of his amen

nearly twenty years before
(which time, not Himmler, had played).
It was winter, but his tomb
wore flowers like an accolade :
they grew there every day.
I came back less afraid.

PEW RENT

How they have changed it all—
the vibrant figure, radiant as a bridegroom,
in the water-glitter ;
the astounding speech, fresh as the blue bloom
on a grape ; the vigour
and spring of it all, lean and vivid as broom.

They have made it a rite
of death : tradition, antiquarianism—
dead images and words ;
history's foxed mirror blurred with chrism,
not seven-splendoured light
streaming magnificently through the prism.

Painfully men have forged
two instruments to be clumsily wise,
two techniques of response :
to legislate, to institutionalize.
Do this to the wellspring
of life, and it dies.

A TOUCH OF WHITE

Six months we lived
on that precipice,
between the wall
and the abyss ;
three of us trapped
upon the ledge
of being, on
the pit's sharp edge.
He was unmoved ;
but sometimes we
glanced sideways down
at the swirling sea,
fathomless white,
of cloud below
and reeled in the rush
of vertigo—
reached out towards
the other's hand
and swayed there on
the heart's last strand.
White drift from
the sea we neared
touched forever
hair and beard.
Feet aslide on
the polished shale,
fingers clawing
the basalt wall,
I sought a sign.
It came like a knock
answered. We stood
on rock.

AFTER AUGUSTINE

So late have I come
to know you, whom I thought
I had known so long.
Every word and report

I had garnered up—
whatever you said
my heart could recall.
Even your bread

you had shared with me.
So long had you been
my nearest neighbour,
it seemed I had seen

to the words' white grain.
Late have I come
to know my ears deaf
and my talking dumb.

I took the truth
for metaphor
until, in the dark,
I beat on your door.

Ask, you had said :
it will be given you.
In agony I asked :
and it was true.

YOURS OF THE 29th

Why Lourdes, not Enlli ? Both
no doubt are places where the earth's
crust is thin, and the world
of grace breaks through. The bedrock girths
are split, and through the dark
fissure refulgence, and rebirths

of limbs and lives, stream down
the serene and innocent air.
Beuno and Bernadette
both saw the true shape that was there,
wholeness and holiness
in form unutterably fair.

Why Lourdes, not Enlli then ?
Not Enlli climbing in a cloud
of light from the green sea,
Enlli untouched, at peace, and loud
only with sea-birds' cries ;
but admass Lourdes, light of the crowd,

spring in the concrete drought
of supermarket, one-way-street,
asylum, city square.
Today a man must go to greet
grace in this wilderness,
the cool cave in this desert's heat.

BILINGUALISM

Athwart the canal, green as Wales,
the great barge drifts. The tow-rope trails
slack in the water. On the bank
the barge-horse grazes, polished flank
turned to the water. Huge as an ark
the barge slides on : its tarred planks bark
the further shore, pointing away
to nowhere in the hot midday.
Browsing on, the indifferent horse
leaves the ark to its calm non-course
as time laps by.

        The problem's how
to turn the horse and the barge's prow
in one direction, harness each
to the other one before this reach
stills to a pool of green pondweeds
and, nose to stern across the reeds,
the barge lies like a monolith,
the stabled horse dies into myth,
means of communication silt
into a water-garden spilt
with dragon-flies, and marsh-worts sway
for picnickers on holiday.

RECONCILIATION

Word over all, said Whitman
and I think so too—
calm, iridescent phonemes
the rainbow curves through,
shibboleth and sesame
understood anew.

Password, too, of our verses—
easing out the nails
of the ancient enclosures,
groping the briared trails
through the old, monstrous forest
hiding Wales from Wales.

CLUES

My poems
are feathers,
drift feathers of doves.

My poems
are slivers
from green olive groves.

My poems
are psalms
for the sun and moon.

My poems
are the talk
of a tongue-tied man.

My poems
are churches,
churches without walls.

My poems
are speeches,
clumsy speeches for Wales.